Yellow Umbrella Books are published by Red Brick Learning
7825 Telegraph Road, Bloomington, Minnesota 55438
http://www.redbricklearning.com

Library of Congress Cataloging-in-Publication Data
Rubin, Alan
  [This farm. Spanish & English]
  This farm/by Alan Rubin = Esta granja/por Alan Rubin.
  p. cm.
  Summary: "Simple text and photos introduce some of the plants and animals raised on farms"—Provided by publisher.
  Includes index.
  ISBN-13: 978-0-7368-6022-2 (hardcover)
  ISBN-10: 0-7368-6022-3 (hardcover)
1. Agriculture—Juvenile literature. 2. Farms—Juvenile literature. I. Title: Esta granja.
II. Title.
S519.R8318 2006
630—dc22   2005025857

Written by Alan Rubin
Developed by Raindrop Publishing

Editorial Director: Mary Lindeen
Editor: Jennifer VanVoorst
Photo Researcher: Wanda Winch
Adapted Translations: Gloria Ramos
Spanish Language Consultants: Jesús Cervantes, Anita Constantino
Conversion Assistants: Jenny Marks, Laura Manthe

Photo Credits
Cover: Gary Sundermeyer/Capstone Press; Title Page: Gary Sundermeyer/
Capstone Press; Page 4: F. Schussler/PhotoDisc; Page 6: Gary Sundermeyer/Capstone
Press; Page 8: Gary Sundermeyer/Capstone Press; Page 10: David Frazier/Corbis;
Page 12: Gayla Sanders; Page 14: Todd Powell/Index Stock; Page 16: Ken
Hammond/USDA

1 2 3 4 5 6 11 10 09 08 07 06

This Farm
by Alan Rubin

Esta granja
por Alan Rubin

Yellow
Umbrella
Books
for early readers

This farm has cows.

Esta granja tiene vacas.

What do we get
from cows?

¿Qué nos dan
las vacas?

This farm has chickens.

Esta granja tiene gallinas.

What do we get
from chickens?

¿Qué nos dan
las gallinas?

This farm has apple trees.

Esta granja tiene manzanas.

What do we get
from apple trees?

¿Qué nos dan
las manzanas?

What else do we get
from this farm?

¿Qué más nos da
esta granja?

Index

Índice